NEWBURY
THEN & NOW

IN COLOUR

DR NICK YOUNG

The
History
Press

The book is dedicated to my parents, Paul and Margaret Young, and to my Nan, Pam Smith, who have supported me as long as I can remember. Also to the memory of my Grandad, Brian Smith, and to my local history mentor, Peter Allen.

First published in 2013

The History Press
The Mill, Brimscombe Port
Stroud, Gloucestershire, GL5 2QG
www.thehistorypress.co.uk

ISBN 978 0 7524 8618 5

Typesetting and origination by The History Press
Printed in India.

CONTENTS

ACKNOWLEDGEMENTS

This publication would not have been possible without the support of a great many people and organisations. Some have loaned me their photographs or given me permission to reproduce them, others have shared their knowledge and provided me with access to various locations to take photographs. A special mention must be made of Laura Connochie, who has proofread, for grammar, many parts of the text; to Tony Higgott, who has painstakingly checked not only my grammar but many of the historical facts of this work; and to Paul Young, who has helped with much of the photography.

The generosity of the people and organisations that have loaned or given me materials, given up their time and shared their knowledge is greatly appreciated. They are: David Canning; Ann and Dennis Clarke; Richard and Barbara Charlton; Laura Connochie; Tony Higgott; Jim Irving; Pam Mills; Dr David Peacock; Jonathan Sayers; West Berkshire Museum; Chris Whitaker; Stuart Wise; Phil Wood; Paul Young; Hallmark Cards; Judges Ltd; Parkway Shopping; Museum of English Rural Life (Reading University); National Railway Museum; Newbury Rugby Club; Newbury United Reformed Church; *Newbury Weekly News*; Oxfordshire History Centre (Oxfordshire County Council); The Francis Frith Collection; The Racecourse Newbury; St Gabriel's School and St Mary's Church (Shaw-cum-Donnington). Apologies to anyone I may have inadvertently missed out.

Every effort has been made to trace copyright owners of materials used within this publication. I sincerely apologise if there are any materials that have been used without acknowledgement, you are, in that instance, invited to contact the publisher.

All of the modern photographs have been taken by myself. Old photographs are credited to those who have supplied and/or taken them; those not credited have been taken either from my own collection, or from the collection of the late Peter Allen.

INTRODUCTION

Newbury is a town full of history, with artefacts including hand axes dating back over 12,000 years to Palaeolithic times, which have been unearthed in the Wash Common area. Other finds dating back to the Mesolithic period were discovered in Faraday Road and Victoria Park. There are Neolithic round barrows in Wash Common, an Iron-Age brooch found at Northcroft, and a Roman cemetery discovered near the present Sainsbury's and Gordon Road area. So, archaeologically speaking, the Newbury area is rich in history.

Despite this, it may be surprising to find that Newbury does not appear in the Domesday survey of 1086. There are entries for Donnington, Speen, Thatcham, Greenham and Ulvritone. You would be forgiven for not recognising the latter; it is believed that Ulvritone would have been situated south of the Kennet. The Domesday Book makes no mention of a church here, although there are churches nearby in Speen and Greenham. Indeed, Ulvritone is noted as having only twenty-two households, small by comparison with its neighbours of Greenham with thirty-four, Speen with twenty-six, and Thatcham with forty-seven. It is thought that the Lord of the Manor at this time, Ernulf de Hesding, who had been given various lands as a result of the Norman Conquest, established a new town. This new town included Ulvritone and extended north of the Kennet, along the present Northbrook Street. The town grew rapidly, eventually overtaking its neighbour, Thatcham, in both size and trade. The new town eventually became known as Newbury and the name 'Ulvritone' disappeared.

During the twelfth century, Newbury was involved in the civil war – the Anarchy – between Stephen and Matilda, with records noting a castle being under siege at Newbury. To this day, the location of the castle remains a mystery and is likely to refer to a timber keep at Hampstead Marshall. By the seventeenth century, Newbury was again involved in a civil war, this time the English Civil War.

This publication shares some of the rich past that Newbury has to offer, highlighting often overlooked and forgotten locations. Some of the old photographs date back over 100 years to 1910 and earlier. All of the old photographs, regardless of their age, have been chosen to highlight the history, but also the changes that have been made. Newbury encompasses a large area; unfortunately, space in this publication is limited and thus there are many views that simply could not be included.

Dr Nick Young, 2013

DONNINGTON CASTLE

DONNINGTON CASTLE, *c.* 1912. The Abberbury family had held Donnington manor from the late thirteenth century. In 1386, Sir Richard Abberbury was granted, by King Richard II, a licence to 'crenellate and fortify a castle on land at Donyngton'. The gatehouse, the only part that remains standing today, dates from this period. There were a total of eight towers around the castle, four round towers on the corners with another two on the gatehouse, and two square towers halfway down the side walls. The courtyard, which measures 20m by 33m, would have contained kitchens, halls and accommodation for guests. Little evidence exists of the interior and structures, which may have been built of timber. The English Civil War broke out in 1642 and by 1643 the castle was in the hands of John Packer, a Parliamentarian. The castle was to play a large role in the war, and after the First Battle of Newbury the castle was taken for King Charles I and subsequently held by a division of the Royalist Regiment of the Earl Rivers, who were under the command of Lieutenant-Colonel John Boys. Boys quickly

enhanced the defences with star fort earthworks surrounding the castle, costing £1,000. The earthworks were to hold gun emplacements, but would also make it much more difficult for opposing forces to get too close to the castle itself. Despite a siege and several attacks by the Parliamentarians, Boys retained control. Eventually, in 1646, under permission from the King, he did surrender the castle. His men were allowed by the Parliamentarians to march down the hill, with full colours and drums beating, heading for Wallingford to rejoin Royalist forces and leaving the castle in ruins. *(Reproduced with kind permission of © Judges Postcards Ltd Hastings www.judges.co.uk)*

TODAY THE SITE is owned by English Heritage, and is Grade I listed and a Scheduled Monument. As can be seen from the photograph (above), the castle has been maintained, foliage has been cleared away and repairs have made over the years. The gatehouse is opened on occasions for people to look inside and the grounds can be visited at any time. The surviving walls give an idea of not only the scale, but the strength and engineering that went into the structure.

DONNINGTON HOSPITAL

DONNINGTON HOSPITAL ON Oxford Road, in around 1905. Following the common custom at this time for the more privileged and wealthy to provide for the sick, King Richard II also granted Abberbury a licence to build a hospital in 1393. The hospital accommodated twelve poor men and a minister, in return for which they were expected to pray for Richard and his family's well-being. The hospital was endowed by the Manor of Iffley in Oxford, which provided an income for centuries to come. The Donnington estate was sold in 1415 to Thomas Chaucer, son of the poet Geoffrey Chaucer, and had various owners until it was in the hands of the Crown by the sixteenth century. In 1551, King Edward VI granted Donnington manor to the then Princess Elizabeth. By the end of the sixteenth century, the hospital was in a poor state of repair and in 1600 Queen Elizabeth I granted the manor to Charles Howard, 1st Earl of Nottingham. Howard sought permission to rebuild the hospital and in 1602 the Queen signed a grant of refoundation. This allowed Howard to rebuild a new hospital on the site, called 'Queen Elizabeth's Hospital'. Like many other buildings, both locally and nationally, the hospital did not

escape the ravages of the English Civil War. In 1645 John Boys, the Royalist commander stationed at Donnington Castle, razed the houses in Donnington village to the ground to deprive the Parliamentarians of any shelter or hiding places. By April 1646, Donnington was once more at peace but the area was in ruins. John Packer, Lord of the Manor before the English Civil War, was returned to his position, and he and his heirs took responsibility for rebuilding the village and hospital.

TODAY THE HOSPITAL, after 600 years, is in itself astonishing and largely thanks to monarchs and landowners who wanted to care for the people on their land. The hospital trust is self-funded, with income to support the hospital coming from the Manor of Iffley and various properties. What were once almshouses today cater for married couples and single men and women of retirement age.

ST MARY'S CHURCH, SHAW-CUM-DONNINGTON

ST MARY'S CHURCH, Shaw-cum-Donnington, *c.* 1909. There has been a church at Shaw-cum-Donnington for over a thousand years. It is known that there was a Saxon church here in around AD 1000. Within the churchyard itself Roman glass vessels and urns were found and other items were discovered a short distance away in Dene Way, indicating that there has been a Roman settlement of some sort in the area. This supports suggestions that Roman tile was used in the construction of the church, although exactly how they were used is unclear. After the Norman Conquest, the tithes were paid to the Abbey of Peraux in Normandy. The rector, Reverand Samuel Slocock, was appointed in 1838, whereupon he is reported to have complained that the church was 'cold, draughty

and uncomfortable.' Slocock suggested to the Lord of the Manor, the Reverend Dr Thomas Penrose, to build a church similar in style to one he had seen on holiday in the Isle of Wight. Penrose gave his permission to do so, thus sealing the fate of the ancient church. Between them they tracked down the architect, Joseph Hanson, to design the new church in the Norman style. The last service in the old church was held on 21st March 1841 and Slocock laid the foundation stone for the new church on 1st June 1841. The Norman Font and a memorial to local clothier Thomas Dolman, who had died in 1711, were saved and transferred from the old church to the new. In addition the bells were also saved, the oldest of which apparently dates to 1631. The new church was consecrated on 6th September 1842 by the Bishop of Oxford. The church continued to expand and in 1878 a chancel was added to replace an earlier and smaller chancel. The church has been expanded even in recent times, one of the changes being the church hall. Although there was a church hall previously, this was rebuilt in 1994 and opened in 1995. *(Photograph supplied by Tony Higgott)*

ST MARY'S CHURCH today, despite these minor changes, looks much the same. That is with perhaps the exception that the secondary school, Trinity, has been expanded to such an extent that it now overlooks the churchyard.

SHAW HOUSE

SHAW HOUSE (RIGHT) in around 1920, before it became a school. The manor of Shaw was purchased in 1557 by Thomas Dolman, a wealthy clothier. Shaw Manor at that time also included two corn mills (Shaw Mills). Upon his death in 1575, Shaw Manor passed to his son Thomas, despite his eldest son John contesting the will. Shortly after inheriting, Thomas Dolman II had Shaw House built, which was completed in 1581. The best guest room is now known as the King Charles Room, but it was previously called the Old Queen's Room. It was named after Queen Elizabeth I, who slept in the room when she visited in 1592. Royal visits continued in 1603, when King James I and Queen Ann visited. Humphrey, son of Thomas Dolman II, inherited Shaw House at the time of the English Civil War in the seventeenth century. The Earl of Manchester sent Parliamentary forces several times to attack Shaw House, but each attempt was successfully fought off by the Royalists. The house was well built and some of the walls were six foot deep, easily withstanding an attack. Local myth says that an underground tunnel

connects Donnington Castle to Shaw House and that it was used during the English Civil War, however, no evidence for such a tunnel has ever been found. At the outbreak of the Second World War, Shaw House was owned by Sir Peter Farquhar and was still a private home. Buildings throughout the area were commandeered for military use, including Shaw House. In 1939, men from the Royal Ordnance Corps trained at Shaw House prior to sailing to France and the house was used throughout the war by the military. Newbury was bombed on 10th February 1943 and several buildings were hit, including St John's Church and the Council School, so the schoolchildren were relocated in May 1943 to Shaw House. The house was later purchased by Berkshire County Council and continued to be used as a school. In 1985, due to safety concerns, the house was deemed no longer fit for this purpose. *(Reproduced with permission from the Museum of English Rural Life, University of Reading)*

TODAY THE HOUSE is run by West Berkshire Council who have offices there and who hold exhibitions throughout the year to allow the public to experience the history of the property, including several discoveries that were only made during the restoration, including a buried kitchen and hidden panelling.

THE FIRS

ORMONDE HOUSE, PICTURED below in December 2001. Originally named The Firs, the house was built in 1861 on land known as Horsepool Field. Within the four acres were gardens, a greenhouse, sheds, other outhouses and a tennis court. In 1901, a John Mason was living there with his family, a cook and a housemaid. In 1905, the

property was bought by John Porter, who was the driving force behind the creation of Newbury Racecourse. He renamed the building Ormonde House, after one of his most successful and loved horses. The property was put up for sale when John died in 1922 and the sale brochure describes the house's modern services including electric lighting, mains drainage, central heating and even a telephone. The house included five bedrooms and another three for servants, two bathrooms, two wine cellars, a dining room, drawing room, kitchen and a library. The property exchanged hands several times before being sold in 1942 to St Gabriel's School for £5,000. They converted some of the outhouses into a church and a gym. The school moved to Sandleford Priory in 1948 and Newbury Technical Institute of Further Education then moved in. In 1951, the institute became the South Berkshire College of Further Education. Ormonde House became the main administrative centre of the college as new buildings were erected over the years to cater for an increasing number of students and a wider choice of subjects. In 1975, it changed to Newbury College and remained in operation on the site until 2002, where, over the summer of that year, it moved to new premises on Pinchington Lane. *(Photograph supplied by Dr David Peacock)*

TODAY THE OLD college site, including Ormonde House, has been demolished to make way for a total of 146 apartments and houses. The main road to the new housing development is called Old College Road and the streets leading off are named after engineers, such as Brunel Court and Telford Court. At the rear of the development is Ormonde Gardens, as a reminder of the original building.

THE TOLL HOUSE

THE TOLL HOUSE (below) occupied by Wells' Bakery, *c.* 1905. The eighteenth and nineteenth centuries saw the rise of Turnpike Trusts, peaking in the 1830s. These Trusts were set up to allow the collection of a toll for use of the road. In turn, the tolls collected were used by the Trusts to maintain the roads. This particular turnpike was part of the Speenhamland to Marlborough Trust, which was set up in 1726, although little improvement in the road condition was seen until 1744. The toll house sits at the junction of three roads: Bath Road leading off to the left, Oxford Road leading off to the right and Oxford Street in the foreground. Bath Road was once one of the main thoroughfares of the town, but has long since been bypassed and is today known as the Old Bath Road. Several other toll houses existed in the area, including near the

Castle Inn at Donnington, Thatcham Gate near the modern Wyvale garden centre, and at Wash Common near the Gun public house. Some of the turnpikes continued running until the 1880s. This house was purchased in 1892 by William Wells, who converted it into Wells' Bakery. William ran it until his death in 1923, after which his wife continued the business. The house was purchased in 1939 by the council so that they could make road improvements. The property stood empty for a number of years prior to its demolition in 1950. Many of the local children believed the house to be haunted, although it is more likely that the sounds they heard were from vagrants occupying the building whilst it stood empty. Besides the bakery the whole area was alive with shops and residential properties. In 1899, shops and businesses in the area included James Wigmore, a grocer and tobacconist; Charles Pearce, a boot maker; John Steptoe, a hairdresser; and Joseph Townsend, a builder and contractor.

TODAY THE TOLL house has gone, but the house behind, The Chestnuts, remains and is now offices. Indeed, most of the area is now occupied by offices. The buildings on the right have been demolished and the area is now occupied by the Job Centre. Further up Oxford Road to the right is now Waitrose.

OXFORD STREET, SPEENHAMLAND

OXFORD STREET AS seen from the Broadway, in around 1910 (right). On the right of the old photograph is York House, originally part of the George and Pelican Inn, and today known as Thames Court. In 1915, James Money, a well-known local architect, was living there. A few doors away is number 4 Oxford Street, originally part of the Bear Inn, built in the eighteenth century. The Bear Inn consisted of several buildings, with the original inn dating to the 1600s. It is said that during the English Civil War, the bodies of three Lords, Carnarvon, Sunderland and Falkland, were brought here from the Guildhall prior to them being taken for burial. Around 1768 the inn was shut and never again reopened as an inn. Further up is the Chequers Hotel, which dates to the eighteenth century. The Bacon Arms is beyond the Chequers and dates to the nineteenth century. In the old photograph it can be seen that they are offering sleeping quarters to members of the Cycle Touring Club (CTC). Both the Chequers Hotel and the Bacon Arms remain to this day and although the two buildings have been altered, some of the original features remain. Next to the Bacon Arms was Gilders Square. Within the Square was the New Theatre completed in 1802 and operated by Henry Thornton. The old theatre presumably was the playhouse in Northcroft Lane, which dates to around 1788. The theatre lasted until the middle of the nineteenth century, after which it closed. However, the building itself lasted until the 1970s, when it was demolished. At the bottom of the road on the left, once stood Holland's the corn merchants, who also owned Greenham Mill. A few doors along was Edward Martins Motor Works, which can clearly be seen in the old photograph with the large 'GARAGE' sign sticking out. Later, the business became Martin and Chillingworth.

TODAY THE LOWER part of Oxford Street looks much the same as it did in 1910, however, the top part has changed significantly. Now there are offices and the Job Centre near to where Gilders Square was. On the opposite side of the road is St Lukes House, which is used as offices.

THE GEORGE AND PELICAN INN

THE PHOTOGRAPH BELOW is looking east along London Road in about 1905, with the George and Pelican Yard on the left. Speenhamland is roughly halfway between London and Bath, and is thus ideally suited for travellers to take a break and stay in accommodation overnight, especially considering the trip would have taken two days at this time. The George and Pelican Inn, on the immediate left, consisted of the George Inn, at numbers 20 and 22 The Broadway, and the Pelican Inn, at numbers 16 and 18 The Broadway and number 2 London Road. The George Inn was rebuilt around 1730 and the Pelican Inn dates to the eighteenth century. Together the two inns are known as the George and Pelican Inn, although many simply referred to it as the Pelican. There are records naming the inn going

back to at least 1646. It is known that Vice-Admiral Nelson stopped there, as well as Queen Maria II of Portugal. It was a coaching inn and operated as such until the 1840s, by which time the railway was taking much of its trade away. The buildings still stand today although they are no longer used as an inn. In the yard – where the sign is in the old photograph – were stables which are said to have been able to hold 300 horses. The Pelican was one of the best-known inns on the main road from London to Bath, but appears to have been expensive. The famous actor James Quin, staying there in the mid-eighteenth century, is credited with etching onto one of its windows: 'The famous inn at Speenhamland that stands below the hill, May well be called the Pelican from its enormous bill'. There were at least nine inns in Speenhamland, and they included the King's Arms Inn, which was built around 1710 and was renamed Dower House. It was used as an antiques shop from about 1910 until about 1952, and stood until around 1960, when it was demolished. Clarendon House, which still stands today, was built in around 1750 as an extension to the King's Arms Inn. *(Photograph supplied by Pam Mills)*

TODAY THE BUILDING that housed the George Inn is known as Thames Court and was also known as York House in about 1900, but there is little evidence that it was once an inn. Various shops have attempted to open along this stretch, but the buildings along this road are largely used as offices.

MARSH ROAD

BELOW IS A view of Park Way from the Forum in around 1972. Marsh Road, now known as Park Way, was created around 1868, and stretched from where Park Street is today to the rear of where Wilkinson now stands. The central parking area and road on the left at this time were still part of the park. To the left of this was a row of trees lining the edge of the Marsh (Victoria Park). It was at this time that Magdala Terrace (Park Terrace) was being created, part of which can be seen in the bottom left of the old photograph. The terrace was named after the Battle of Magdala in 1868 and consisted of twelve houses facing onto the Marsh. Access from Northbrook Street could be made

through Alton Place. Alton Place was altered during the 1880s, and some of the workshops and houses where demolished to create Park Street; in addition, Magdala Terrace was renamed Park Terrace. Marsh Road was extended north in the 1930s to connect to London Road and around the 1920s it was suggested that a bridge be built to connect to Wharf Road, but this idea was dismissed. At the same time the road was widened by taking land from the park. The trees were removed, some of the houses in Park Terrace demolished and the eastern (left) part of the road created. A bridge was created during the Second World War and initially only pedestrians were allowed to use it. This is the layout that is shown in the old photograph. The Forum Cinema was also built in the 1930s, and it is the roof of that building where the photograph is taken from. The Forum has gone through several owners and names, including ABC, Robins, and Cannon. By the 1990s, the cinema was no longer drawing the crowds it once did and it closed in 1998. Although suggestions were put forward to build a new multi-screen cinema on the same location, the building was bought and turned into LA Fitness, which was later replaced by Nuyuu Fitness. (*Reproduced with permission of* Newbury Weekly News)

THE MODERN PHOTOGRAPH shows Park Way viewed from the London Road. Nuyuu Fitness has itself been replaced by Énergie Fitness Club. The road and car park in the middle has been replaced by the Parkway development, which was officially opened in 2011, although building work continued into 2012. Parkway consists of a shopping centre with stores including Debenhams, John Lewis, Cath Kidston and Costa. On the upper floors of the development are residential properties, and below the complex is underground car parking. Sadly, the view of the Town Hall clock tower and St Nicolas' Church from ground level has been obscured by the Parkway development.

THE GREYHOUND

THIS PHOTOGRAPH (RIGHT), taken around 1960, shows
London Road with the Greyhound pub on the left and the
Handy Stores. Shaw Road can just be seen on the left of the
photograph and on the right, just out of view, was the original
Robin Hood pub. The Robin Hood was a private house in 1817
– when there are records of a change of ownership – and had
become a beerhouse by 1839. It is not known when the house
was erected, likewise with the Greyhound and Handy Stores.
The Greyhound, also a beerhouse, is noted in the 1851 census
and also appears to have had a brewery, which was operated
in 1865 by Henry Reynolds. Shaw Road was, and still is,
lined with Shaw Crescent, also known as Smith's Crescent.
This is a terrace of two-storey houses built around 1823.
Shaw Road had at least three pubs, including the Old Dog, the
Wheatsheaf and the Cock Inn. The whole area including part
of Shaw Road and London Road, going up to the White House
(now the Narrow Boat), was part of Speen parish and known
as Woodspeen East. It became part of Newbury in 1878. The
1960s saw many of the buildings in the area demolished,
including some of the terrace in Shaw Road, the Greyhound
pub, the Handy Stores and the Robin Hood pub. A roundabout
was then constructed which connected Shaw Road, Western

Avenue and London Road. It was later extended to connect the A339, which itself was extended both north and south of the roundabout. Slightly further to the east, just past the Robin Hood pub, thus avoiding demolition, is Myrtle Cottage. It was purchased in order to be used as a replacement for the original Robin Hood. Myrtle Cottage was built before 1837 and is a three-storey semi-detached villa. Further to the east, roughly opposite where Faraday Road is now located, once stood a silk factory. *(Photograph by Jim Irving)*

IN TODAY'S PHOTOGRAPH, the Greyhound, Robin Hood and Handy Stores all stood to the left of the current pub. The Robin Hood pub has survived, although not in its original location and is now a Toby Carvery. The traffic has increased significantly. The modern photograph shows a wider area than the old photograph and the extent to which changes have been made.

THE CLOCK HOUSE

THIS OLD PHOTOGRAPH shows the Jubilee Clock in around 1900, before the construction of the Clock House, which now stands out as a prominent feature in the Broadway but is a relatively recent addition. On a map drawn by John Willis in 1768, the location is labelled 'The Chapel Houses' which appear to have been built on the site of an ancient wayside chapel that, possibly around the time of the Reformation, stopped being used as such. The houses were demolished for reasons unknown in 1791 and the site was then vacant for over thirty years. Speenhamland Lamp was erected in 1828 and consisted of a stone column with a gas lamp at the top. The column is believed to have been donated by Frederick Page from his quarry near Bath and gas was supplied from the newly opened Newbury Gas Works. The stone column was moved in 1888 to the junction of the Old Bath Road and Speen Lane, to make way for the construction of a clock to celebrate Queen Victoria's Golden Jubilee. The Jubilee Clock, as shown in the old photograph, was erected in 1889 and paid for by public subscription. It stood some 36 feet high and had two drinking fountains. Originally, four gas lamps branched off the supporting columns, but later they were replaced by the free-standing lamps

shown in the photograph. A Russian gun, presented to the borough after the Crimean War, was placed with the clock. Later the gun was moved to the Marsh (Victoria Park) where it remained until the Second World War, when it was melted down at Plenty's iron works, giving three tons of good quality metal. The Jubilee Clock was replaced in 1929 with the Clock House. Within the shelter is an inscription: 'This Clock House was the Gift of James Henry Gooding, 1929. Builder E.B. Hitchmam, Architect C.R. Rowland Clark'. The structure itself is hexagonal, but the clock has three faces; one to face into each of the roads adjoining it (on the Broadway): Oxford Street, London Road and Northbrook Street.

TODAY, THE CLOCK House is well maintained, but no longer forms a roundabout where the A4 and A34 crossed. One side has seen the road replaced with a pedestrianised area, making it much safer for people to look at it, but also protecting it somewhat from passing traffic. Rarely is it referred to as the Clock House, today most people call it the Clock Tower.

JOSEPH HOPSON & SONS

THIS BEAUTIFUL OLD building (right) housed Joseph Hopson &
Sons, and is on the corner of Northbrook Street and West Street,
photographed around 1899. This building, numbers 64 and
65 Northbrook Street, was erected in 1877. The 'Swiss–Mauresque'
building replaced an earlier Georgian building and Joseph Hopson
set up shop there in 1854. An advert in 1858 clearly identifies
the business address as Northbrook Street, although it did extend
down West Street. The same advert in *Blacket's Newbury Guide*
describes Joseph Hopson as a photographic artist, but also selling
rugs, carpets, table covers and blinds. Joseph was one of the first
professional photographers in Newbury, if not the first, however,
by 1863 he was trading solely in furniture and upholstery. In
1920, Joseph's grandson, Paul Hopson, married Norah Camp, the
daughter of Alfred Camp, another businessman and originally from
Barnstaple in Devon. One year after the wedding, the two businesses
merged to form Camp, Hopson & Co. Ltd, known today simply as
Camp Hopson. The building later became home to Halfords and was
demolished in 1969, to be replaced with the building that stands
there today. The road to the right is West Street. It is thought that
Bartholomew Street was once known as West Street, as being the

other road to the west of Cheap Street. An auction held on 3rd April 1849 at the Pelican
Hotel in Speenhamland sold off lots in what was to become West Street. Included in the
auction was the building shown on the right of the old photograph, today McDonald's.
Further down the road, the auction guide states that for some of the lots purchasers
'may cover over the stream or watercourse at the back of their lots'. West Street not
only had residential properties but also a school, dispensary, and many more businesses.
(Photograph supplied by Tony Higgott)

TODAY, MOST OF the shops have gone, but the new building is now home to Waterstone's.
Many businesses, including Halford House Dental Practice and Newbury Snooker Club,
are still based in West Street, along with car parks and residential properties. The 'Swiss–
Mauresque' building has disappeared, but the stone carving that was on the West Street side
of the building remains.

JACK OF NEWBURY'S HOUSE

JACK OF NEWBURY'S house (right) in around 1913. Until recently, John Smallwood had long been accepted as 'Jack of Newbury' and many associate this house with him. However, research conducted by Dr David Peacock has shown otherwise and it is believed that he originally came from Barking in Essex, and not Winchcombe in Gloucestershire, as has been propagated in local histories for a considerable time. Documentary evidence notes his father-in-law as Michael Winchcombe, the meaning of father-in-law being a stepfather rather than the modern meaning of the term. Hence his name is often written as John Smallwood alias Winchcombe, or more commonly just Winchcombe. John Winchcombe I was based in Newbury by about 1500, where he leased various properties and lands in the area. His son, John Winchcombe II, is the celebrated Jack of Newbury. John Winchcombe II like his father was a clothier, but unlike his father he gained immense wealth and owned vast properties, including the manors of Thatcham and Bucklebury. It is not known when the house here was built, but it is generally assumed to be around 1500. The original house was built

around two courtyards with frontage on Northbrook Street that stretched at least 29 metres, from Marsh Lane to Jack Street, and perhaps beyond. The house stretched back towards the Marsh (Victoria Park) and extended in excess of 29 metres. By 1736, the house had been split up into shops with one becoming the Jack of Newbury Inn, which is known to have existed on the site from around 1754. Sometime after 1765, a large part of the house was demolished and was replaced with a Georgian building that was to become the Jack of Newbury Inn, and later the Jack Hotel. It is unknown why it was demolished and rebuilt, but may have been due to fire damage, as evidence of fire is still visible in what remains of the original structure. *(Reproduced with kind permission of © Judges Postcards Ltd Hastings www.judges.co.uk)*

TODAY THE ALLEYWAY, Marsh Lane, has changed little. The remaining part of the original house, number 24 Northbrook Street, is now occupied by Monsoon. Parkway shopping complex has since been built over much of where the rear of the house would have been. The frontage onto Northbrook Street shows little signs of its origins. Although some of the original house has survived, it is sad to see such an historic building going largely unnoticed by all those who pass it.

THE
JACK HOTEL

THIS PHOTOGRAPH (RIGHT), taken in around 1928, shows the Jack Hotel on Northbrook Street. Looking north along Northbrook Street, the Jack Hotel at No. 22 is the most prominent building. According to its brochure, the building was built in 1500 and was the Jack of Newbury Inn by 1754. The inn and subsequently the Jack Hotel were named after Jack of Newbury, who today is believed to have been John Winchcombe II. The inn and hotel occupied part of what was once Jack of Newbury's house, some of which still exists further down the street at the corner of Marsh Lane and which is today Monsoon. It is said that Jack of Newbury entertained King Henry VIII and Catherine of Aragon at his residence. By 1928 the stables at the rear had given way to garages. The hotel, under the management of Horace Cadd, was closed and demolished in 1934 to be replaced by Marks & Spencer,

which remains in the same location today. The origin of the road name, Northbrook Street, remains one of debate with local historians, some suggesting that the name dates back to the fifteenth century and so-named as the road was north of the brook, the brook being the River Kennet. Others suggest that it may have simply been 'North Street' and the 'brook' added later, referring to the ditch that once ran along the west side of the road. The name is most likely to have come from Speenhamland Water, which ran across the road where the Broadway and Northbrook Street meet. Hence the road that runs north to the brook or to the north-brook – 'Northbrook'.

TODAY THE STREET has been pedestrianised and shops still populate it. Rather sadly though, some historical buildings have disappeared in order to make progress! However, Camp Hopson is still trading after 100 years, which is a remarkable accomplishment and a credit to both those managing it and to the town.

THE UNITED REFORMED CHURCH

THE CONGREGATION CHAPEL (right) pictured around 1865. The Reverend
Benjamin Woodbridge was well known locally for his involvement with the
Independent Movement in Newbury, which he got involved in after leaving the
Church of England in 1662. After Woodbridge died in 1684, the congregation split in
two, the Independents and the Presbyterians. By 1686, the pastor of the Independents
was Benjamin Merriman. They shared the meeting room, apparently a barn that once
stood near the present chapel, until 1697. At this time the Presbyterians moved to
a newly built chapel (the minister of which was William Taylor) which stood where
Waterside Youth Centre now stands. The Independents remained in their chapel at
Cromwell Place. Merriman took many of his old congregation with him to the new
movement. The Independent Movement is known to have been present in Cromwell
Place since at least 1687, where they were using a converted barn. The yard was
known as Union Place before 1815 and the Independent Chapel Yard after that. It
became Cromwell Place in 1878 and retains the name to this day. A new chapel was
built in 1717, which was subsequently replaced with another chapel building in
1822. A schoolroom was built in 1856 on the site where nine cottages once stood at
a cost of £1,757. The church was then enlarged in 1872. The chapel had become a

Congregation Chapel in the early 1800s and was then demolished in 1958, and a modern replacement was completed a few years later, which became a United Reformed Church in 1972. Six cottages on the south side, before the schoolroom, were owned by the United Reformed Church and one of these was home to Invicta Bookshop, which opened in 1969. They were sold in 2010 to a developer and converted into residential properties. *(Photograph supplied by Newbury United Reformed Church)*

THE UNITED REFORMED Church has today seen the graveyard, grass and trees replaced by a car park. The church is still used and is home to many events, including antiques fairs and talks. It is comforting to know that something historic, namely the schoolroom, has survived but sadly, being situated down an alleyway, the church and other buildings go largely unnoticed.

CAMP HOPSON
AND WOOLWORTH

NORTHBROOK STREET IS home to many historic buildings and businesses. Perhaps two of the most recognised in the southern part of the street are Woolworth and Camp Hopson, pictured below in Northbrook Street in 1960. Woolworth arrived in Newbury in the 1920s and sold nothing that cost more than sixpence. The chain was established in America by Frank Winfield Woolworth with his first store – the forerunner to what would become Woolworth's – opening in 1879. In 1909, Liverpool became home to the first store outside of America and was known as the 'Threepence and Sixpence'. The chain

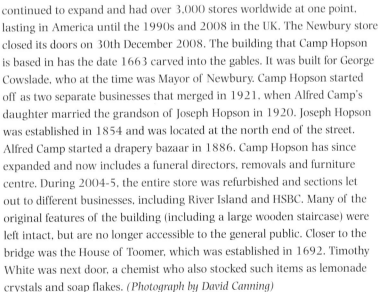

continued to expand and had over 3,000 stores worldwide at one point, lasting in America until the 1990s and 2008 in the UK. The Newbury store closed its doors on 30th December 2008. The building that Camp Hopson is based in has the date 1663 carved into the gables. It was built for George Cowslade, who at the time was Mayor of Newbury. Camp Hopson started off as two separate businesses that merged in 1921, when Alfred Camp's daughter married the grandson of Joseph Hopson in 1920. Joseph Hopson was established in 1854 and was located at the north end of the street. Alfred Camp started a drapery bazaar in 1886. Camp Hopson has since expanded and now includes a funeral directors, removals and furniture centre. During 2004-5, the entire store was refurbished and sections let out to different businesses, including River Island and HSBC. Many of the original features of the building (including a large wooden staircase) were left intact, but are no longer accessible to the general public. Closer to the bridge was the House of Toomer, which was established in 1692. Timothy White was next door, a chemist who also stocked such items as lemonade crystals and soap flakes. *(Photograph by David Canning)*

TODAY CAMP HOPSON survives, is still a department store and is still managed by the same family. Sadly though, few other businesses from even fifty years ago remain in this part of Northbrook Street. The building that previously housed Woolworth's stood empty for a period, but is now home to Wilkinson.

THE MARSH

VICTORIA PARK LOOKING west in around
1960 (right). Local legend tells that the marsh
was given to Newbury by 'two maiden ladies'.
This may be a myth, but it indicates the Marsh's
ancient origins and, indeed, Neolithic flint tools
were found in the Marsh during construction of
the boating pond. The marsh was common land
up until the 1930s and was used in the past for
peat extraction, grazing and the drying of cloths.
John Winchcombe and other clothiers dried their
cloths there, resulting in the nickname Rack
Marsh. The Marsh was used during the English
Civil War, where earthworks were created and
troops were drilled. Cricket was being played on
the Marsh by 1791 – which was then referred to
as Newbury Marsh – and pony racing and other
sports also took place there. In 1838, a row of
poplar trees was planted to commemorate the
coronation of Queen Victoria. The two main
footpaths were erected in the 1880s and lined

with lime trees and seats. The Marsh was renamed Victoria Park upon the death of Queen Victoria in 1901. The statue of Queen Victoria was moved from the Market Place to Victoria Park in 1966. Improvements to the park were made in the 1930s and the park was officially reopened in 1935 on the Silver Jubilee of King George V. In 1936 Park Way was created, resulting in trees and land being removed from the park and taken up by the new road. (*Reproduced by kind permission of the David Canning Collection.*)

THE PARKWAY DEVELOPMENT towers over Victoria Park today, but the bowling green, rebuilt club house, bandstand, boating pond and tennis courts remain. The park is still popular for events, but the Newbury skyline has been forever changed by the looming building that holds the shopping complex.

HAM MILLS

HAM MILL AS seen from the Kennet and Avon Canal around 1933 (below). The mill was once part of a large estate known simply as Ham. In the eighteenth century, the estate was owned by the Croft family of Thatcham. Until the twentieth century, Ham was part of the parish of Thatcham. The original Ham Mill was located to the north of the present mill, near where Newbury Manor Hotel is today. This mill (north) was powered by the River Lambourn and is confirmed in Willis' map of 1768. Until the eighteenth century, documents simply referred to Ham Mill but within the eighteenth century there are several variations on the name. An agreement from 1764 between Ann Cooke and Joseph Newton records 'Ham Mills', whilst Willis' map of 1768 has 'Ham Mill'. It is likely that this is because the mill had more than one grindstone and hence the plural mills. In the 1790s, reference is made to 'Ham or Dyer's Mill' – in 1793 land in Ham was owned by

John Dyer and his son, presumably this would have included the mill, and it was therefore referred to as Dyer's Mill. However, by 1826 most documents refer to Ham Mills Estate, rather than Ham Estate. The enclosure map of 1815 clearly shows two separate mills: the north mill and the south mill (pictured), and are collectively called Ham Mills. Each have their own buildings, including millers' cottages. The first Ordnance Survey map of 1881 clearly identifies Ham Mill as the south mill and simply records the north mill as 'Corn Mill, disused'. The north mill became a sawmill known as Ham Saw Mills sometime between 1881 and 1899. It was later demolished and Newbury Manor Hotel built.

TODAY THE ORIGINAL Ham Mill (north) has gone and it is the south mill, which still stands, that is referred to as Ham Mill. The building looks similar to how it did ninety years ago, although the buildings have been modified and it is no longer a working mill. There is little evidence of the original mill left, and none at all of the stocks and the whipping post that once stood, since at least 1691, near Ham Mill Bridge.

THE WHARF

THE WHARF ON the left, as seen below in around 1910, is famed for being the site of Newbury Castle. Newbury Castle is associated with the civil war between Empress Matilda and King Stephen. During this time the castle was held for the Empress by John Marshal when, in 1152, it was besieged by King Stephen, but no evidence has been unearthed by excavations to support the claim that a castle once stood here. It is more likely that Newbury Castle is actually one of three castle mounds at Hampstead Marshall, which was owned by John Marshal. The Kennet Navigation was completed in 1723 and connected Reading to Newbury. It was at this time that the Wharf was created, along with the basin, where boats could be loaded and unloaded. This stretched a great distance to somewhere near the granary. Buildings were erected around the site, including warehouses and

workshops. The canal was extended until in 1810 it became the Kennet and Avon Canal, connecting the Thames to Bristol. It is around this time that a weighing shed appears to have been erected. The basin was partially filled in during the 1920s and completely in the 1930s. The old photograph shows Kendrick House on the left, known today as Wharf House. This west (left) side dates to the eighteenth century, whilst the east (right) side dates to the nineteenth century. To the right can be seen some of the storage sheds which were used by Dolton's corn merchants. Dolton's were established by 1845; their storage shed survived until the 1920s. On the right is a wooden bridge that crossed a stream which once ran around the Marsh (Victoria Park). The Wharf has since been used as a bus station and car park.

THE WHARF IS now home to two car parks, a taxi rank, a toilet block, Newbury Library and West Berkshire Museum. The crane has been replaced with one that was salvaged from the Great Western Railway's goods yard; although no longer used; it is one of the few reminders of some of the industrial activity that once went on in the area.

THE PRESBYTERIAN CHAPEL

THE PRESBYTERIAN CHAPEL can be seen in the background of this old photograph, taken around 1900. The congregation had broken in two in 1684, but they continued to share the same chapel. Before this, the Presbyterians and Independents were one congregation with a chapel in what is today Cromwell Place. In 1697, the Presbyterians had a new chapel built, shown in the centre of the old photograph, and moved out of the old chapel leaving the Independents there. Inside the chapel was a gallery, a pulpit and seating facing north. Much of the original interior still remained in 1900, although some items had by necessity been repaired or replaced, whilst others had been disused for some time. By 1768, maps show a stream going off to the right of the chapel

from the river and an alleyway leading all the way from the chapel back to Northbrook Street. Near to where the photographs were taken stands a bridge. During the Second World War, concern grew over there being only one main route through Newbury and that it may be a target for bombing. The main route at the time was the A34, which crossed the river over the bridge at the southern end of Northbrook Street. Plans and ideas were made that included a swing bridge and a lifting bridge, but the construction met with further delay when financing was considered. The Ministry of Transport wanted Berkshire County Council to pay for half the cost of construction, but they saw no reason why they should pay for something that was for military use. Eventually the War Office ordered the construction of a temporary bridge and paid the full cost of construction, which was completed in 1940.

THE PRESBYTERIAN CHAPEL was demolished in 1960 and has been replaced by the Waterside Youth Club, and a new bridge was built when the original was dismantled in 2001. The youth centre was designed by Patrick Sweetnam and building work was completed in 1964. To the right in the modern photograph, just out of view, is the rear of Camp Hopson, which now has a large furniture store that opened in 1998. The buildings on the left of the photograph have also been demolished to make way for a car park.

THE BRIDGE

THE BRIDGE OVER the River Kennet as seen in around 1933 (right). A bridge has existed in this location since before 1623, when the then wooden bridge, which had shops on either side of it, collapsed into the river. A replacement wooden bridge was erected, but was swept away in floods in 1726 and yet another replacement was erected shortly after. In 1769, work began to replace the wooden structure with a more solid stone bridge which was completed in 1772 and still stands today, although there have been repairs, some of which can clearly be seen by the new, brighter stones. Other changes include lamps that were added in the centre of the bridge, one on either side on the balustrades, but removed some time after the Second World War. The current bridge has endured much over its long history. Until the end of the 1970s, two-way traffic flowed over the bridge

including passing double-decker buses, which must have left little room for pedestrians. It has borne other heavy loads, including on one occasion a low-loader lorry that was carrying a train. Although the bridge supported the weight, the lorry became stuck on the hump. The Globe Inn, dating back to 1611 and possibly earlier, stood on the south-west side of the bridge, but closed around 1870 (the white building on the right of the modern photograph). In 1879, it was purchased and used as the 'Old Bank', which was then sold in 1895 to 'Capital and Counties Bank'. In 1918, this was absorbed into Lloyds bank, now Lloyds TSB, who remains in the premises to this day.

LIDDIARDS BUTCHER'S, WHICH was on the north-east side, is today the West Cornish Pasty Company. Another recent addition is The Lock, Stock and Barrel pub, which opened in 1993 and is on the left of the modern photograph. The right-hand side shows a different story, where a building is being constructed on what was once the gardens of the Globe Inn. Besides Lloyds TSB still being present, it is nice to see Griffins, the family butchers, on the south-east side, who have been operating on the same site since 1856.

LOCK KEEPER'S COTTAGE

MANY WILL RECALL the Lock Keeper's Cottage, which once stood near the Kennet and Avon Canal. There were, as seen in the old photograph below from around 1950, two houses, the one with skylights and the one behind it. English Heritage noted that in surveys, the buildings had many openings that had been blocked up and it has been suggested that they were once used as a mill. It is unknown when the buildings were erected, but English Heritage has documents saying both the eighteenth and nineteenth centuries. If it was once a watermill, it is likely to have been built prior to the canal. It was not until the 1790s that work started on extending the canal west, to connect the Kennet Navigation to the Avon Navigation at Bath. Two men are often noted in connection with the building of the canal, John Hore with the Kennet Navigation and John Rennie with the later extension that was completed in 1810,

when the canal became the Kennet and Avon Canal. The canal was successful; however, with the coming of the railway in the middle of the nineteenth century, the canal started to decline. Despite this, some continued to use it commercially until about 1950, when a stretch near Woolhampton became unusable; thus severing the link with Reading. One person who continued to use the canal was John Gould, who was actively involved in getting the canal restored and as such became, in 1948, secretary to the Kennet and Avon branch of the Inland Waterway Association (IWA). The Newbury branch broke away from the IWA in 1951 to form the Kennet and Avon Association, which later became the Kennet and Avon Canal Trust. In 1989, the Lock Keeper's Cottage burnt down. Due to the work of Gould and others, the canal was officially reopened by the Queen at Devizes in 1990. In recognition of his contribution Gould was awarded an MBE in 1992. *(Copyright The Francis Frith Collection)*

TODAY, THE OUTLINE of the Lock Keeper's Cottage is marked out in brick, an information panel is placed nearby and a plaque erected to Gould. There is plenty of seating on the site of the house, allowing people to sit and watch the boats go through the lock.

TOWN AND WEST MILLS

ALMOST EVERY OLD settlement will have a mill and Newbury is no exception, with West Mills seen below in around 1955. The Domesday record shows that Newbury, then known as Ulvritone, had two mills, most likely to have been on the sites of the Town Mills and West Mills. Originally, both are likely to have been corn mills, but as cloth industry became important, the three mills at West Mills all became fulling mills. West Mills is to the left of the old photograph, with Town Mills behind the tree in the centre. The area around took its name from West Mills as did the road leading from Bartholomew Street. In his book *Newbury Road by Road*, Roy Tubb suggests that it was also known as Globe Lane after the inn which once stood on the corner of Bridge Street, where Lloyds TSB now stands, though this may only have applied to the section around the north side of St Nicolas' Church. Hovis Ltd owned both Town and West Mills from 1921 to 1957, when H. Dolton & Sons Ltd purchased them.

West Mills was later used as a furniture store by Windsor & Neate, but in 1965 it burnt to the ground. Trencherwood Estates Ltd later purchased the property and in the early 1980s, it was redeveloped into seven dwellings called Dolton Mews, and in 2004 Island Cottage was built, replacing an earlier building of the same name. Town Mills was sold to a property developer in 1972 and the buildings were demolished. The site remained vacant for some time and throughout the 1970s several ideas for its redevelopment were reported in the *Newbury Weekly News*. These included plans by Newbury District Council to turn it into a canal-side amenity area; this proved quite popular. Other ideas were to use it as a car park, a hotel, or residential housing for the elderly. Finally, Trencherwood Estates Ltd purchased the land and in the early 1980s erected two buildings containing twenty-one apartments. Further along the south side of the canal there are three cottages set at right angles to the road. These were almshouses established by Thomas Hunt in 1729, though the current building dates from 1817. Nearer to the swing bridge are almshouses established by the wills of Thomas Pearce in 1671 and Francis Coxhead in 1690. *(Photograph reproduced by kind permission of Hallmark Cards)*

TODAY, THE PEARCE and Coxhead buildings are now occupied by Horsey Lightly, Solicitors. The canal is used by barges, mostly for pleasure, and many people enjoy sitting by the canal for a break, especially those who work in or near the town.

WEAVERS' COTTAGES AT WEST MILLS

THE WEAVERS' COTTAGES originally consisted of seven dwellings and date to the seventeenth century, though they are shown below in around 1933. The cottages themselves underwent several changes; in the 1790s beams in the cottages were cut to allow for chimneys to be added and to provide accommodation for navvies. Although the canal, in the form of the Kennet Navigation, came to Newbury in 1723, it was not extended through West Mills until the end of the century. The six-mile stretch from Newbury to Kintbury of what was to become the Kennet and Avon Canal, opened in June 1797 and reached as far as Hungerford by 1798. However, the complete Kennet and Avon Canal did not open until 1810. The ground to the north of the cottages was raised

in order to contain the canal. The Great Western Railway bought the Kennet & Avon Canal Company in 1852. The company, in 1877, made a loss for the first time and in 1920 commercial navigation ceased. The condition of the canal declined, as did that of the cottages which were later, in the 1950s, sold to Newbury Borough Council for £600. Archibald James Campbell Cooper and Gertrude Elizabeth Bazett converted the cottages into two houses in 1963. During the conversion some of the original features, such as the windows and doors, were removed. From somewhere in this area, on 2nd July 1816, William Plenty launched his first lifeboat. This particular boat was christened *The Experiment*. The boat was sailed from somewhere in West Mills to Reading, and then on to London Docks. William came from Southampton so it may be his time spent there that inspired his creation of such a boat, although the timing with the opening of the Kennet and Avon Canal could also be a factor. The boat was very successful and saw many of them deployed around the coast.

TODAY LITTLE HAS changed, visually at least. Many of the properties have been converted into residential use and a few new buildings have been erected. Internally though, the properties have been altered, although as many of them are listed buildings the alterations have been done in a way that attempts to preserve their original features.

ST NICOLAS' CHURCH

ST NICOLAS' CHURCH, seen here on the right in around 1910. The Domesday survey makes no mention of a church in Ulvritone, which was at that time smaller than the neighbouring Speen, Greenham and Thatcham. Ulvritone was noted as having only twenty-two households compared to thirty-four in Greenham, twenty-six in Speen and forty-seven in Thatcham. Following the survey, it is thought that the new lord of Ulvritone, Ernulf de Hesding, decided to establish a new town. There is evidence that a church was in existence by 1085, although the exact details are unknown, meaning that a church has existed on the site of the present St Nicolas' for over 900 years. Through the years, various noblemen were in charge of the church, including Sir Lewis Clifford in 1394 and Sir Thomas Erpingham in 1404. As with most churches, the wealthier parishioners paid for building extensions, such as Robert Bullock, who founded a chantry in the church in about 1330. Between 1509 and 1520, the church was entirely rebuilt with credit, according to Thomas Fuller's *History of the Worthies of England*, largely due to John Winchcombe I. Fuller states that Winchcombe 'built the church of Newberry, from the pulpit westward to the tower inclusively'. Winchcombe's son, also John, continued to support the building of the church. It is believed that the new church was completed in 1532, with all traces of the former church destroyed. In 1922, a memorial was erected in memory of those who lost their lives in the First World War. The monument was officially dedicated on 1st October 1922, with a service attended by an estimated 8,000 people who gathered in the churchyard and streets surrounding the monument. It stands some 17 feet 6 inches tall and was a joint effort by St Nicolas' Church and the town. As seen in the modern photograph, it was erected on the north-east corner of the church and opens out to the street rather than into the church, to avoid connection to any specific denomination and be freely accessible to the public.

TODAY, THE CHURCH remains active and open to the public, holding many events including heritage open days. Most, if not all, of the old monuments inside the church survive, such as that of John Winchcombe I, located at the bottom of the tower.

THE TOWN HALL AND MANSION HOUSE

THE TOWN HALL and Mansion House are often confused as being the same building. Mansion House is the building on the right of the old photograph, taken around 1881. It was built in 1742 and designed by James Clarke, who also designed the bridge over the Kennet, just a stone's throw away. The building was used as a base for the borough council, but primarily provided a large function room for the town and use for social events, including balls, banquets and even theatrical performances. At one time it was known as the Newbury Assembly Rooms, being fitted out to a high standard, with elaborate chandeliers and large paintings. Cooking apparatus was fitted in the basement to provide for various events, including the Mayor's inauguration dinner. The open ground floor of the building formed the shambles, used for the sale of meat, fish and dairy products on market days. The Town Hall is the building fronting onto the Market Place, incorporating the two towers. Designed by James Money, brother of the local historian Walter Money, the hall was built by 1878, although one of the towers was increased in height in 1881 to allow a clock to be added. The design is influenced by that of Reading Town Hall, where the architect was Alfred Waterhouse. The total cost of the building was £4,345. By the early 1900s, the narrow Mansion House Street was limiting the flow of traffic and it was decided that it should be widened. In 1909, the Mansion House was demolished and an extension to the Town Hall was built in 1910, to provide additional space for the Borough Survey and other officers. The building was known as the Municipal Offices and was about a third narrower than the Mansion House. A drinking-water fountain that had been presented by Thomas Fidler in 1859 was incorporated into the new building in virtually the same position. *(Reproduced with permission of Oxfordshire History Centre, Oxfordshire County Council)*

THE TOWN HALL looks almost the same today as it did 100 years ago, and still houses Newbury Town Council and other organisations. The road surface has been paved with brick and is pedestrianised, although only between certain times.

THE MARKET PLACE

THE MARKET PLACE (below) looking toward Mansion House Street with the statue of Queen Victoria, taken after 1903. The historic Market Place has seen a significant amount of change during its history, and yet in photographs and paintings it is always reassuringly recognisable, regardless of the date. A market cross once stood here indicating where the market was held and is known to have been in existence since 1205, but may be older considering that in about 1160 the men of Newbury attacked the market at Thatcham. Furthermore, the name of the town itself, 'New Borough' (Newbury), suggests that it is probable that Newbury had a market, or fair, in about 1080, around the time Newbury was established. One of the characteristics of a borough is that it is a trading settlement. In the centre of the Market Place once stood the Guildhall, later referred to as the Old Town Hall. It is believed to have been rebuilt or extended in around 1611, but originating from around 1485. By the early 1800s the building had become dilapidated and it was demolished in 1827. A statue of Queen Victoria was erected in 1903 and was presented to the town by

George Sanger, a circus showman who was born in Newbury. The statue had four lions which stood on top of a large plinth and was moved to Greenham House in 1933 and later, in the 1960s, to Victoria Park. Only two of the four lions were placed in Victoria Park and only recently have the other two been placed back at the Queen's feet.

TODAY THERE IS still a market, which has now been in existence for at least 800 years. The Market Place remains a centre for many of the events that take place, including the Christmas lights being turned on, events organised by the Corn Exchange, and celebrations, such as the Olympic Torch passing through. Many will remember The Plaza – its entrance passageway, as well as surrounding buildings (behind the camera), have all been demolished. The Kennet Centre, on the left, saw several properties demolished at about the same time. The Plaza and the former Dreweatt's buildings were all demolished around twenty-five years ago, and new offices for Dreweatt's (now Carter Jonas) built on the site.

CLOTH HALL

THE CLOTH HALL (left) prior to restoration, around 1899. Newbury once had a booming cloth industry with several notable clothiers, including John Winchcombe I, John Winchcombe II and Thomas Dolman. By the seventeenth century the cloth industry was in decline, with many of those who had worked in the industry now jobless. In 1624, John Kendrick, a clothier from Reading, left money in his will to allow for premises to be purchased so that those who had lost work could be employed. At this time neither the Wharf nor Wharf Street existed, so access to the Cloth Hall would have been from King's Road. The building, erected around 1627, was a courtyard arrangement but today the only part left is the museum. The building had seventeen rooms including a dye room and one called the 'Chamber'. The latter was heated, one of only two that were. By 1673 it had become a workhouse that included a hospital with a resident doctor. In 1706, the Chamber was used as a school, but by 1722 the school had relocated to the Temperance Hall. The east and west wings were demolished by the middle of the nineteenth century, and the south wing – now the museum – was used as a corn store. John Rankin, Mayor of Newbury from 1899 to 1901, purchased the building in 1902. With the aid of public subscription he restored the building, in memory of Queen Victoria, which was then presented to the Corporation. The weather vane was placed on top of the building in 1902 and is a replica of an earlier one, originally a green dragon, which is said to have

come from the Guildhall. The museum held a small collection of artefacts, but the official museum opening was not until 1904, when it opened as the Museum of Antiquities and Natural Curiosities. The museum's core collection came from the Newbury Literary and Scientific Institution. *(Photograph supplied by Tony Higgott)*

AT THE TIME of writing, the museum is undergoing restoration and is due to reopen in 2014. Since 2007 the museum has closed and reopened a number of times for essential health and safety improvements. In October 2010, the museum closed its doors for redevelopment, and the artefacts were started to be packaged and sent for storage.

THE CORN EXCHANGE

THE CORN EXCHANGE (right) prior to its 1980s restoration
(*c.* 1962). The exchange of corn most likely took place in the
Market Place until the Corn Exchange was erected. Building of the
Corn Exchange (seen on the right in the two photographs) started
in 1861 based on designs by the Reading architect J.S. Dodd.
The building was opened to the public in June 1862. Essentially
the building was just a large hall and had agricultural-related
advertising around the hall. Not only was corn traded, but there
was also a wool market and the occasional sale of livestock. The
large hall provided space for events other than trade and one
such event was held in 1863 to celebrate the marriage of Albert
Edward and Alexandra of Denmark, the Prince and Princess of
Wales. The celebrations were held all over Newbury, with sports
and amusements in the Marsh (Victoria Park) and a dinner for
400 people at the theatre in Speenhamland. Other commodities
were also traded, especially as the corn trade started to decline,
including oil, insurance and farm machinery. There were

suggestions in about 1909, when Mansion House was being demolished, of using the Corn Exchange as the Town Hall. The building was renovated in the 1950s and by the 1960s was being used on a regular basis for music events starring such acts as The Who. There was also roller skating, public meetings and dramatics in the building. The building closed to the public in about 1988 due to concerns over safety and after a £3.5 million refurbishment, it opened to the public as a professional theatre with 400 seats in 1993. In 2000, the ownership of the Corn Exchange was passed from West Berkshire Council to the Corn Exchange Trust, thus becoming an independent body. *(Photograph by Augustine Letto, supplied by Jonathan Sayers)*

TODAY, THE CORN Exchange has its own small cinema called 'Screen One'. The cinema shows the most recent films and amateur dramatics continue, including *Cinderella* and *Animal Farm*. There are also regular comedy shows from the likes of Chris Addison and Lucy Porter. The Corn Exchange receives over 100,000 visitors a year and by any measure is a true success. The Hatchet Hotel is today owned by Weatherspoon's and is known as The Hatchet Inn. Likewise, the Queens Hotel, shown on the right in the photographs, is owned by Marston's Inns.

BARTHOLOMEW STREET

THE ROAD WAS known in the fifteenth and sixteenth centuries, and possibly earlier, as West Street, being the road to the west of Cheap Street. Eventually though it became known as Bartholomew Street for being the road that led to St Bartholomew's Hospital, and is shown below looking north in around 1933. The Regal Cinema can be seen on the left and was built on the site of the Red Stores, who stocked toys, books and gramophones. The Regal opened on 4th April 1931 and lasted until 1963. The cinema, together with other properties including that of W. Burton (at 11A), Heathers Stores (at 12 and 13) and Bendy's Stores (at 14 and 15) were demolished to make way for Pearl House, which was built in 1966-67. This was an office block that reached several stories high. The top floors were demolished in 1999, but the lower floors remain. On the opposite side to the Regal Cinema is the Bricklayers' Arms, a nineteenth-century

public house. The pub has gone by several names including the Rat and Parrot, the Bricklayers, the Purple Lounge, and is today called The Newbury. Another pub on the east (right) was the Falkland Arms, near to which was Herborough House, which was once the home to local historian Walter Money and later became Nias Garage. Both buildings, along with many others, were demolished in the 1970s, some earlier, to make way for the development of the Kennet Shopping Centre. Once there was an alleyway that led to the back of the Catherine Wheel public house (now the Jack of Newbury) in Cheap Street. Just behind where the photographer is standing once stood B&Q, which later became Poundland and more recently was home to the George and Pelican pub.

THE STREET HAS now been pedestrianised from the junction with Market Street. The George and Pelican now stands empty, and the east side of the street is lined with the Kennet Shopping Centre and its multi-storey car park. Some of the older, historic buildings have survived, but many go unnoticed with the Kennet Centre being the focus of many visiting this end of the town.

CHEAP STREET

CHEAP STREET LOOKING north in around 1908 (right), which extends on to the Market Place and back to Winchcombe Road, has been in existence since at least the fifteenth century. The road has had various spellings over the years: Chepyngstrete in 1439, Cheapestrete in 1453 and Cheape Street in 1584. The name 'Cheap' would have referred to a place to trade, hence the original name referring to 'trading street'. The road leading to the left is Market Street with its cobbled entrance. Approval to create Market Street was given in 1869, along with a new cattle market which opened in 1873. The New Market Inn (later known as Newmarket Inn), seen on the corner of Market Street, was built in about 1869, perhaps its name coming from the new cattle market. The building survived until the 1970s, when several properties were demolished and replaced by car parks, shops and eventually the Kennet Shopping Centre. The Catherine Wheel, which is in the distance, beyond the lamp post in the modern photograph, is an eighteenth-century building and was renamed in 2010 the Jack of Newbury, not to be confused with the old Jack of Newbury Inn that was once in Northbrook Street. There was no shortage of pubs in the area;

others within Cheap Street include the Axe and Compass and the Weavers' Arms. Further down Cheap Street, just on the right past the corner, once stood Kimber's Almshouses. John Kimber, who was Mayor of Newbury in 1758-59, left in his will money to allow for the creation of almshouses for six men and six women. He died in 1793, and the executors were quick to find land and erect a building, which was completed in 1795. They were in use until the 1940s, after which replacement houses in Kennet Road were being used. The almshouses stood empty and were demolished in the 1950s.

TODAY, THE NEW Market Inn has been replaced with the Vue Cinema, a multi-screen complex that opened in 2007. Excavations undertaken prior to the cinema identified several structures and wells, some dating back to the twelfth century. The road layout has been altered with Cheap Street now being effectively broken in two as the main traffic route swings into Market Street.

MARKET STREET

MARKET STREET, SEEN on the right in around 1988,
connects Cheap Street to Bartholomew Street, and, as
its name suggests, it once had a market there. Prior
to 1873, the sale of sheep and cattle took place in the
yards of inns between Cheap Street and Bartholomew
Street. This was not always convenient and suggestions
for a new cattle market had been made in 1869;
shortly after that plans were put in place to create
one. It was decided that a new road should be created
for access to the market and thus land was acquired
to allow the creation of Market Street. The new cattle
market was opened in 1873 and was located where
the bus station is today. Despite being called a cattle
market, pigs, horses and sheep were also sold there, as
often highlighted in the adverts printed in the *Reading
Mercury*. The market proved popular and was extended
in 1915 and modernised in 1953. Unfortunately, this
success did not last and the market closed in 1969.
At this time, the whole area was undergoing changes

with the initial development of the Kennet Shopping Centre. Opposite the cattle market stood Victoria Place; the houses were demolished at this time and Sainsbury's supermarket took their place. The cattle market site was then used as a car park until 1973, when Newbury District Council decided to build a multi-storey car park. The building work was completed in 1975, as can be seen in the old photograph. The multi-storey lasted until the end of the 1980s, when it was demolished and turned into a bus station. In 1982, Newbury District Council, today known as West Berkshire Council, moved into newly built offices to the south-west of the multi-storey. (*Photograph taken by Jim Irving*)

TODAY A BUS station remains with no trace of the original cattle market. A multi-storey car park exists at the western end of the road and the new Vue Cinema complex has been erected and opened (2009) on the corner of Market Street and Cheap Street (right foreground).

ST MARY'S HOSPITAL

CHEAP STREET BELOW in around 1967. The hospital, dedicated to St Mary Magdalene for women with leprosy, was established by 1232 and it is assumed that this is the building on the left behind the iron railings. In 1375, a deed records a house named the House of Blessed Mary, which is generally thought to be the forerunner to what became St Mary's Almshouses by 1604. At the same time, in 1604, Frances Winchcombe made provision for the poor at the almshouses. St Mary's Almshouses also went by the name of Old Maids Almshouses and were for six poor women. This part of the road was for a time known as St Mary's Hill, after the almshouses. The building shown was constructed in

1864, with three sides surrounding a courtyard and whitened walls. Behind the building was St Mary's Court, which was demolished early in the twentieth century. The almshouses were demolished in about 1970 and new ones were erected in Derby Road. The site was redeveloped into Mill Reef House, a four-storey building, which was built for Newbury District Council, who operated there from 3rd February 1975. They moved to new premises in 1982 in Market Street where they remain today, although now known as West Berkshire Council. The Empire Café, which opened in 1947, is a few doors away and is still operating today. On the right was Newbury Free Library which opened in 1906 in purpose-built premises. The library remained until 2000, when a new building was erected in the Wharf. The building is now occupied by Prezzo restaurant. *(Photograph taken by Jim Irving)*

TODAY SEVERAL OF the old buildings including the almshouses have gone; however, many others like the old library and the King Charles Tavern remain standing. Shops such as T4 cameras and Empire Café remain trading, although no doubt they have been affected by the larger chains now operating in the town. There are several pubs, including the Diamond Tap and the King Charles Tavern.

NEWBURY RAILWAY STATION

THE GREAT WESTERN RAILWAY (GWR) had been operating from London to Bristol since 1841, but did not come to Newbury until 1847. It opened on 21st December as a branch line from Reading to Hungerford and was later extended to Westbury, and then on to Penzance. A Roman cemetery was uncovered during the construction of a goods yard, indicating that there may have been some Roman occupation in the area. There are two other Roman cemeteries in the area, one found in Shaw churchyard and another at Salcombe Road. One of the first items to be carried by train was coal, which was used by the Newbury Gasworks to produce gas, and was previously carried on the canal. The railway signalled the start of the end of the canal, although it did not happen overnight. The railway gradually started to carry more and more goods that were once moved on the canal. Expansion continued with the Didcot, Newbury and Southampton line. Newbury railway station itself, shown below in the old photograph looking east in

around 1919, was altered in 1882 and 1900, with a complete rebuild between 1908 and 1910. Despite this early success, it was not to last; passenger traffic stopped on the Didcot-Newbury-Winchester line in the early 1960s, and closed completely a few years later. The railway, like the A4 and A34 roads, gave access to almost anywhere in the country with relative ease.

TODAY, UNLESS YOUR destination is on the main line, there is a strong chance you will have to travel to another station, such as Reading, and change. Branch lines have been removed and the goods yard has long since gone. However, the station building itself looks much the same today as it did 100 years ago, with the exception of the modern ticket machines.

RAILWAY BRANCH LINES

THE MAIN RAILWAY line from London to Bristol bypassed
Newbury in 1841. Had Newbury been on the earlier route it
may have helped the town's trade to grow, and increased its
chances of capturing more trade from London and Bristol. The
old photograph (right) shows the main line to Reading with the
Didcot line on the left. Construction of any railway rarely went
smoothly and the Didcot line was no exception. The *Illustrated
Police News* of 3rd September 1881 reported an accident
involving eight men working on the line. The men were riding
on a ballast truck when the engine suddenly fell on its side,
pulling the truck with it. The men were thrown from the truck,
one reportedly ending up under the engine. Boiling water was
ejected from the engine and the men were scalded; one so
badly that the bone could not be set. Two of the men sustained
severe injuries, including broken bones. The *Leicester Chronicle*
reported that one man was so seriously injured that it was
unlikely he would recover. A large event, organised by Mayor
Mantagu Palmer and local historian Walter Money, marked the

opening of the Didcot line on 12th April 1882. A procession that included a detachment of the Berkshire Yeomanry Cavalry, Woodspeen band and the band of the 93rd Highlanders marched from the Market Place to the railway station. The timing was such that as the procession reached the station the first train would arrive from Didcot. The line was then officially declared open by Lady Loyd Lindsay. The old photograph shows *Cornish Rivera Express* being pulled by a Warship class engine, going past Newbury East Junction signal box on 23rd March 1960. *(Photograph by David Canning)*

TODAY, BEHIND THE camera, is the Sterling Industrial site which was former home to Sterling Cables, the tower of which is still present. The Didcot line has been removed, having been closed in the 1960s. Raceview Business Centre and Mandarin Court now occupy land on the left, where the junction box and Didcot line once were. In the distance, the Racecourse railway station still exists and is used regularly. The view is set to change though, with the electrification of the line.

THE NEWBURY MARTYRS

THE NEWBURY MARTYRS site, The Sandpits, is pictured below in around 1935. Queen Mary's reign (1553-58) was wrought with religious persecution. Mary, being a devout Catholic, saw it as her duty to return England to the Catholic faith. Thus, in her bid to save England, she needed to rid the country of heretics. Although other monarchs before and after did this as well, none did it to the same scale, with some 238 heretics being burnt at the stake during her reign. The people of Newbury were affected by this persecution, but three Protestant men in particular; Julius Palmer, Thomas Robyns (also known as Thomas Askew) and John Gwyn, who were tried on 15th and 16th July 1556. The trial took place at St Nicolas' Church, with judges consisting of Dr William Geoffrey, who was representing the Bishop of Salisbury, John Winchcombe II (also known as Jack of Newbury), Sir Richard Brydges, Sir William Rainsford and Reverend Clement Burdett. They were convicted, essentially, for heresy and treason. At 5 p.m. on the second day, Sir Richard Brydges and the bailiffs of the town, together with a company of harnessed and weaponed men, escorted the

three men to a site known as Sandpits in Enborne Road to be burnt at the stake. The three men went to the stake and kissed it. They were then bound to the stake, after which Palmer said to the watching crowd: 'Good people, pray for us that we may preserve unto the end, and for Christ his sake beware of Popish teachers, for they deceive you'. As he spoke, one of the bailiff's servants threw a faggot (a bundle of twigs or sticks) at him, cutting his face. For tormenting Palmer the sheriff hit the servant on the back of his head with a walking stick so hard that his head began to bleed. After the fire had started to take hold, the men apparently raised their hands towards heaven and started to speak: 'Lord Jesus, strengthen us, Lord Jesus, assist us, Lord Jesus, receive our souls'. It is doubtful that they could have continued this for long before the pain became too much. The exact location is not known, but the general area is thought to be somewhere on the north side of Enborne Road, between numbers 5 (The Lamb pub) and 11. *(Reproduced with kind permission of © Judges Postcards Ltd Hastings www.judges.co.uk)*

THE AREA IS now a large residential development, with The Lamb pub nearby. The only evidence of the burning is a small monumental inscription outside Newbury Hall. An event such as this serves as a reminder of how restricted people were in their religious views, how swift and cruel punishment could be, and also the amount of freedom we have today.

ARGYLE ROAD

ARGYLE ROAD IN the snow (right), around 1950. On the left-hand side, halfway down, is St Bartholomew's Hospital, which was erected around 1200. A grant from King John in 1215 allowed the hospital to hold an annual two-day fair on the day of St Bartholomew and the following day in August. The fair was held in Fair Close, with the money raised going to support the almshouses. On the right in the foreground is Litten Cottage (Bartholomew Manor), which was built in the sixteenth century and leased to John Winchcombe I and John Winchcombe II. A little further down on the same side, where the Raymond's Almshouses stand, stood a large brick shed used for animals and storage, which was probably built for John Winchcombe II. St Bartholomew's Hospital was rebuilt around 1618. Around 1670, twelve almshouses replaced the shed and were built for Philip Jemmet. His estate later passed to his son-in-law, Sir Jonathan Raymond, and his

grandson, Sir Jemmet Raymond. Thus the almshouses became known as Raymond's Almshouses. In 1878, the road had officially become Argyle Road, previously it had been known as Wash Lane. Dr Walter Essex Wynter moved to the house in 1919 and after finding a reference to the propoerty as 'Bartilmewes', renamed it Bartholomew Manor. In 1929, Dr Wynter rebuilt Raymond's Almshouses and gave them to Middlesex Hospital for the use of retired nurses. St Bartholomew's Hospital became known as King John's Almshouses. Likewise, Raymond's Almshouses have been known by several names, including Church Almshouses, Gladstone Cottages and Raymond's Cottages.

TODAY THE ROAD looks much the same, indeed without the cars it would look very similar to how it did 100 years ago. New buildings have cropped up at the end of the road, mostly in Derby Road, and many of the buildings have been renovated, all in keeping with their original character.

ST JOHN'S CHURCH

THE PARISH OF St John the Evangelist was formed on 25th October 1859 and comprised of parts of the parish of Newbury and Greenham. A church was erected and consecrated on 17th July 1860 by Dr Samuel Wilberforce, Bishop of Oxford. William Butterfield was the architect who designed the church. He had designed several other buildings, including the vicarage and St Nicolas' School in Enborne Road. Finance for the building of the church came from Miss Ellen Hubbard and was done so in memory of her parents, John and Marion Hubbard. The church, as can be seen in the photograph below (*c.* 1910), stood on the corner of Newtown Road and St John's Road. Reverend Thomas Hubbard was the first vicar of the church. The church could seat 500 people. Little changed until 10th February 1943 when a lone German bomber, who was probably targeting the railway line, dropped its load, directly hitting St John's Church and completely destroying it. Other nearby buildings were also damaged or destroyed, including St Bartholomew's Almshouses, the council school and Southampton Terrace. The latter is where the small garden is now on the opposite side

of the road to the church. Some fifteen people, including children, died as a result of the attack and a further twenty-five needed hospital treatment. The bombing happened at 4.45 p.m.; had it been any earlier the casualties would have been much higher. An altar was erected on Sundays at St John's day-school, to allow for the service to take place and the daily Eucharist was done in the vicarage. A temporary church was erected in 1944, but it was not until 1946, when the Reverend Pritchard became vicar, that plans started developing for the building of a new church. The Ministry of Transport acquired some of the land from the church to allow for the construction of a roundabout and footpaths, so the new church could not be built in exactly the same location. It was also required that the new church be set back from the road. There were minor issues in the planning stage, but these were soon overcome and planning permission was given. HRH Princess Margaret laid the foundation stone of the new church on 13th April 1955. The church was completed in 1957 and was dedicated by the Lord Bishop of Oxford on 13th June 1957.

THE CHURCH REMAINS today, although the surrounding area has changed, not least of which with the demolition of the London Apprentice, which stood just to the left of the photographs. The pub had been on the site from the seventeenth century, but was demolished in the 1950s as part of the development of the area. In recent years cycle tracks, seen in green, have been added.

NEWBURY GRAMMAR SCHOOL

NEWBURY GRAMMAR SCHOOL (right) as it appeared
in around 1910. Henry Wormstall is often credited
with the founding of Newbury Grammar School in
1466. He did indeed leave, in his will of 2nd May
1466, property for trustees to establish a chantry in
the parish church of Newbury (St Nicolas' Church).
A chantry means that a priest is endowed to sing
Masses for the founder, Wormstall in this case, and for
all departed Christian souls. There is no evidence that
Wormstall intended for the priest to teach, although
he did stipulate that the chantry could be altered,
and when teaching actually started and by whom,
is up for debate. The dissolution of the chantries
is the first evidence that confirms the presence of
a schoolteacher that most local historians agree
on. It was the dissolution of the chantries that saw
commissioners being dispatched in 1548 to locate
them, and value and seize them. Land and tenements
associated with Wormstall's chantry were seized

and granted away by the King to John Knight, Robert Were and others. An exception was made as the exchequer paid the schoolmaster, Thomas Evans, £12 per year to continue his teaching. The house that the schoolmaster was living and teaching in was also seized as it was part of the chantry. The townspeople provided him with another schoolroom, a chapel known as the Litten, in the ancient hospital of St Bartholomew. Student numbers dropped to just three in 1798 and no students at all in 1800. The situation did not change until the 1840s, when the trustees agreed to attempt to revive the school. Work soon started on rebuilding the Litten and the school opened in August 1849. Permission was given in 1880 to create new buildings on fields next to Enborne Road and construction started in 1884, with the school opening on the new site on 28th July 1885. There was space for over 100 boys. In 1975, the school merged with Newbury County Girls' Grammar School, located a short distance away, and together they became St Bartholomew's School.

TODAY MUCH HAS changed. In 2006, permission was granted to redevelop the entire school, which opened in 2011. As a result, some of the school properties have been sold. The old St Bartholomew's school building, Wormstall's site as it was known, has been developed into flats as part of the St Bartholomew's Grange development by Linden Homes. In September 2011, the school gained 'academy' status and, at the time of writing, has 1,650 students aged eleven to eighteen.

GIRLS' HIGH SCHOOL

THE EDUCATION ACT of 1870 created school boards that
were tasked with supplementing the church system of
schools and by 1881 there was sufficient resources to allow
the government to make attending school compulsory for
children aged five to ten. However, girls still did not have the
same opportunities or quality of education as boys and the
Girls' School was established to change this. The Newbury
Technical Institute building, together with an adjoining
house, The Limes, were leased – the latter was initially
used for boarding. Miss Esther Jane Luker was appointed
headmistress and the school opened on 20th September
1904 with thirty-nine pupils. The intake increased rapidly
from sixty-six in 1905 and ninety-four in 1906. There were
so many pupils that the boarding house was moved in 1909
to Bartholomew Farm and the old boarding house was used
as classrooms. The problem was recognised in 1907 and
so plans were made to move the school to a purpose-built
location. The site chosen for the new school was on the
corner of Andover Road and Buckingham Road. The new
school, as seen in the old photograph in around 1926,
was opened on 29th September 1910. Although there was

development on the other side of Andover Road, the area around Buckingham Road was largely undeveloped at this time. By 1914 there were only three pupils using the boarding house and it was closed as it was no longer financially viable. Overcrowding continued to be an issue with further problems in the 1930s when the school had over 300 pupils; the number was added to by fifty evacuees and later a further 400 evacuees, together with additional staff. The latter 400 evacuees from the Godolphin & Latymer School in Hammersmith had use of the school in the afternoon, and the Newbury pupils had use of it in the morning. In 1945, the name was officially recorded as Newbury County Girls' Grammar School. Proposals and preparations for amalgamating the Newbury Grammar School with the Girls' High School were proceeding at the start of the 1970s, and included the fact that the new amalgamated school would be a mixed comprehensive catering for ages eleven to eighteen. The amalgamation was completed in 1975 and the school became known as St Bartholomew's School.

THERE HAVE BEEN many changes over the years and in 2006 permission was granted to redevelop the entire school. The redeveloped school opened in 2011, but as a result some of the school properties have been sold. The old Girls' School has, as of 2012, been developed into flats and is now part of the St Bartholomew's Grange development by Linden Homes.

NEWBURY RACECOURSE

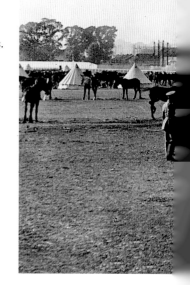

AN ARMY ENCAMPMENT at Newbury Racecourse in 1914.
Horse racing took place in Newbury as early as 1738 at Wash
Common. A few races were recorded and it is likely that racing
continued, although it was not officially recorded again until
1805. Two-day race meetings were held from 1805 to 1811
in Enborne, but were described as 'Newbury Races' on event
calendars. These meetings comprised a grandstand as well as
additional entertainment, including cockfighting and theatricals.
In 1811, the land was set to be enclosed and racing was moved
to Woodhay Heath in Hampshire. In 1815, racing was held
both at Woodhay Heath and at Northcroft Meadow, with the
latter also called 'Newbury Races'. Both events took place in
September, a week apart from each other, but it is unknown if
these were related or independent events. The following year
racing at Woodhay Heath, the official race meet, seems to have
stopped. The idea for a racecourse in Newbury was discussed
locally in the 1890s, with credit for the initial idea going to the
Duke of Westminster. However, despite the owner of Greenham
Lodge, Lloyd Baxendale, having a course laid out on his land,
the plan was dropped and it was not until John Porter got
involved that progress was made. That said, the licence was

delayed due to issues regarding the Jockey Club and it was only following King Edward VII's involvement that it was finally approved. The Newbury Racecourse Company was formed and shortly after, in September 1905, the first race meet took place at the newly constructed racecourse. The opening race was won by Copper King, with Charles Trigg in the saddle. Racing continued until September 1914, when it was abandoned due to the outbreak of the First World War. Some racing took place in 1915 and 1916, but was again stopped in 1917 and did not restart until after the war. Prisoners of war were held at the racecourse from September 1914 and guarded by reserves. Reports of the numbers vary from 600 to more than 3,000 people being held there. By the end of December 1914 they had all been moved elsewhere. Racing resumed at the end of the war, but stopped again at Easter of 1940, due to the Second World War. The racecourse was handed over to the American Army in 1942, and was used as a depot and marshalling yard. Racing once again resumed in 1949. *(Photograph supplied by Tony Higgott)*

TODAY THE RACECOURSE remains a popular destination for horse racing, in addition to other events such as music concerts. In September 2012, the racecourse changed its name from 'Newbury Racecourse' to 'The Racecourse Newbury'. This rebranding is in part due to a partnership between the racecourse and David Wilson Homes. The latter is responsible for the new housing development consisting of about 1,500 homes.

NEWBURY
DISTRICT HOSPITAL

NEWBURY DISTRICT HOSPITAL (below) as it was in around 1905. The hospital, designed by Mr H.G. Turner, was opened on 18th November 1885 to meet the needs of the district. Before the hospital, there was access to medicine through the Newbury Dispensary where the 'better off' paid an annual subscription and poor people could approach subscribers for a ticket, which would allow them to be given treatment. Financing of the building of the hospital was by voluntary subscriptions. A total of £5,600 was raised, £1,000 of which was given by Major Thurlow of Shaw House. Land belonging to St Bartholomew's Charity called Horse Fair Close was purchased and the hospital built upon it. The hospital was originally built with capacity for twelve patients, and was for the treatment of non-infectious diseases and accidents (a hospital

built at Wash Common in 1893 dealt with infectious diseases).
Expansion included a new ward, Victoria, in 1894 and additional
nurses' accommodation was added in 1901. By 1907, a children's ward
had been added and in 1914 a new wing was added that consisted of
offices, a waiting room and two wards. By 1915 there were thirty-four
beds and by 1942 there were 130 beds. The hospital was used for
military patients during the First and Second World Wars. During the
1930s the hospital was remodelled and continued to expand. In 1948,
the newly formed National Health Service took over the hospital, but
private patients were still accepted. By the end of the 1990s, plans
had started for selling the hospital site for development and building a
new hospital. Sovereign Housing purchased the land for £5.1 million
and in September 2004 had approval to erect eighty-five sheltered
accommodation units. Building started in September 2005, finished in
March 2007 and was named 'Carnarvon Place'. The hospital itself was
relocated to the present site at Benham Hill, Thatcham, which opened
in 2004.

TODAY THE NEW Sovereign Housing development is in full use.
Off-street parking keeps the main road clear and the new hospital is
well situated. Many had thought it would include an accident and
emergency department, and that it would also integrate the maternity
unit from Sandleford Hospital, but sadly these services are located
some distance away at Reading and Basingstoke hospitals.

THE ROKEBY ARMS

THE FOURTH BARON Rokeby, Matthew Montagu, lived at Sandleford Priory with his aunt, Elizabeth Montague. He died in 1831 and it is around this time that the first Rokeby Arms was opened, named after him. It is likely that a private house already existed on the land and simply opened as a beerhouse. One of the first landlords, in 1837, was John Durbridge, who remained as landlord for forty years. One of his successors, Ralph Ernest Thorn, became landlord in about 1913. He was a stonemason previously and may well have continued working as such as well as being a landlord. In addition, Ralph was also a member of the Newbury Volunteer Fire Brigade. He was called to action in 1916 and saw his first major offensive in France during 1917. This was successful, but upon his return to camp a German shell exploded and killed him. The original pub was demolished around the 1930s and a new purpose-built pub was erected, as shown in the old photograph (c. 1960).

Originally, the building was number 143 Newtown Road, but renumbering of the area put it at 101 Newtown Road. The new pub was larger, presumably as it was attracting more customers from the passing cars for which it was well situated. At this time Newtown Road would have been the main way out of Newbury if travelling south. In 1997, there was a suspected arson attack on the building and just two years later it was demolished to make way for a new development, Grove Court. Nearby and on the opposite side of the road was the Newbury Union Workhouse, which was completed in 1836. As a Union workhouse it served several local parishes. A separate infirmary with twenty-two beds was built in about 1837 and the workhouse itself was extended in the 1840s. It continued as a workhouse into the twentieth century. It later became Sandleford Hospital and was incorporated into the National Health Service in 1948. (*Photograph supplied by Paul Young*)

TODAY THE ROKEBY Arms has been demolished and replaced with a residential development called Grove Court. After the new hospital opened in Turnpike Road in 2004, Sandleford Hospital was demolished for development and replaced with Jago Court, also a residential development, with over 100 dwellings.

WASH COMMON

THE NORTHERN END of Wash Common as seen in around 1905 (below). The First Battle of Newbury took place in the area in 1643 and is shown by the many roads named after people that took part in the battles. One such road is Essex Street, which commemorates Robert Devereux, Third Earl of Essex, who commanded the Parliamentarian army in the First Battle of Newbury on 20th September 1643. The area has been known as Wash Common since at least 1774, but has also been referred to as simply 'The Wash'. The pub seen in the centre of the photographs is The Gun. There has been a pub on this site since at least 1761, when documents refer to the 'Gun at Wash Gate'. The pub was owned in the 1800s by Hawkins & Canning of Newbury Brewers. The Falkland Memorial was erected in 1878 and unveiled in September of that year, by the Earl of Carnarvon. It is built of Cornish granite weighing 40 tons and stands approximately 33 feet high. The

original intention was to commemorate all those who fell in the First Battle of Newbury. However, members of the committee and the Earl of Carnarvon wanted it to be a memorial to the Royalists and have nothing to do with the Parliamentarians. The inscription on the monument makes mention of Lucius Cary, Viscount Falkland, for his part in the battle. The farmhouse of Falkland Farm, which used to stand where Falkland Garth is now, is reputed to have been where Lord Falkland's body was taken after his fatal attack against the Parliamentarian forces.

TODAY THE ROADS have been straightened and roundabouts added. Shops and flats have been erected to the west (left) of The Gun, but the monument itself remains, although the lead lettering has disappeared. The monument is noticed by all that go past it, but few know why it was erected and the full history of the area.

SANDLEFORD PRIORY

SANDLEFORD PRIORY AS a private residence in around 1899 (below). It was built in about 1200 for Augustine monks, although there is evidence to suggest that the site was already inhabited before the priory was built. It was established by Geoffrey, Count of Perche. Permission was given for a mill to be built near the Enborne River and, in addition, the priory was allocated an income from the Town Mills. By about 1440, the priory was in a ruinous state and the then prior, Simon Dam, was deposed because of this. Sadly, his successors were unable to recover the priory to its former glory. Towards the end of the fifteenth century, it came into the hands of the Dean and Canons of Windsor, who appear to have let the property out for use as a farm. Sandleford was part of the manor of Ulvritone (Newbury) until the seventeenth century, when a dispute was raised which, when resolved, saw Sandleford become a parish. The priory had various owners, including Edward Montague. In 1780, five years after Edward's death, the property was extensively

renovated by his wife Elizabeth, *née* Robinson. The remodelling was in the Gothic style and undertaken by James Wyatt, with landscaping by Capability Brown. Many of the original timbers still remain despite this extensive renovation. Elizabeth was involved in the 'Blue Stocking' society and entertained friends at both Sandleford and their London home. After Elizabeth died in 1800, the property continued to pass through various hands until an Anglican community of nuns purchased it in the late 1940s; the estate was broken up at this point and some of the land was divided. The nuns bought it for use as a school, namely St Gabriel's, initially established in 1929 as an independent school for girls. Before moving to Sandleford Priory, the school was located for a period at Ormonde House on Oxford Road. *(Photograph supplied by Tony Higgott)*

TODAY SANDLEFORD PRIORY is still St Gabriel's School; however, some of the former land, now Sandleford Park, has been earmarked for the development of a new housing estate. The school is a registered charity and the building retains its character, although changes continue to be made, such as the addition of new buildings. The school caters for all ages, accepting pupils from three to eighteen years. Despite being a girls' school, a small number of boys have also attended; five out of 477 in 2010, all of whom were in the early years' foundation stage (three to five years old).

If you enjoyed this book, you may also be interested in ...

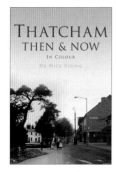

Thatcham Then & Now
DR NICK YOUNG

Tracing the changes and developments that have taken place in the historic town of Thatcham during the last century, *Thatcham Then & Now* captures the essence of the town and its people by comparing forty-five rare archive images of the area with the same scenes of today.

978 0 7524 6276 9

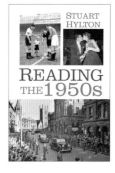

Reading: The 1950s
STUART HYLTON

Reading: The 1950s is a fast-paced and entertaining account of life in Britain during an extraordinary decade, as we moved from post-war austerity to the swinging sixties. There are dramas, tragedies, scandals and characters galore, all packaged in an easily readable 'dip-in' format.

978 0 7524 9353 4

Berkshire Folk Tales
DAVID ENGLAND & TINA BILBE

These lively and entertaining folk tales from one of Britain's most ancient counties are vividly retold by local storytellers David England and Tina Bilbe. Their origins lost in the oral tradition, these stories from across Berkshire reflect the wisdom (and eccentricities) of the county and its people.

978 0 7524 6745 0

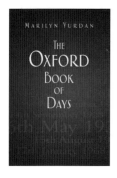

The Oxford Book of Days
MARILYN YURDAN

Taking you through the year day by day, *The Oxford Book of Days* contains quirky, eccentric, amusing and important events and facts from different periods of history, many of which had a major impact on the religious and political history of Britain as a whole.

978 0 7524 6550 0

Visit our website and discover thousands of other History Press books.

www.thehistorypress.co.uk